RALPH KOLTAI

RALPH KOLTAI

DESIGNER FOR THE STAGE

with an Introduction by TREVOR NUNN

Edited by Sylvia Backemeyer

NHB Nick Hern Books

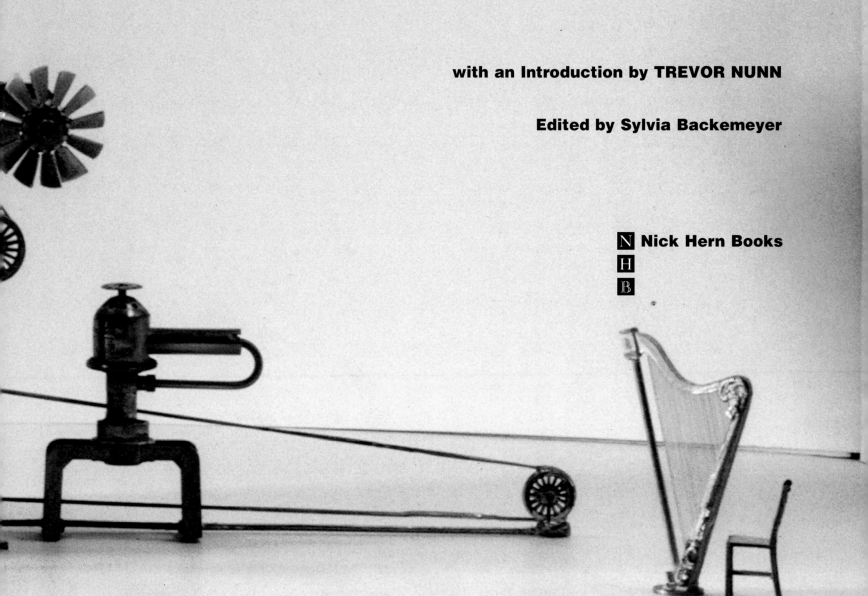

First published in Great Britain in 1997 by
Lund Humphries Publishers
in association with
The Lethaby Press

This third revised and expanded edition
published in Great Britain in 2003
and distributed by
Nick Hern Books Ltd
The Glasshouse
49a Goldhawk Road
London W12 8QP
www.nickhernbooks.co.uk

British Library Cataloguing in Publication Data
A catalogue record for this book is available from
the British Library

ISBN 1 85459 784 1

Designed by Chrissie Charlton & Company
Made and printed in Great Britain by
BAS Printers Limited, Salisbury, Wiltshire

ACKNOWLEDGEMENTS

I should like to take this opportunity of thanking everyone
who helped me to produce this book: the Ballet Rambert,
the Britten-Pears Library, the Chichester Festival Theatre,
the English National Opera Archives, the London Borough of
Islington, the Old Vic Theatre, the Royal Opera House
Covent Garden, the Royal Shakespeare Company, Scottish
Opera, the Theatre Royal Stratford East, the Victoria and
Albert Theatre Museum; and David Brook, Fenella Fielding
and Malcolm Stewart.

Sylvia Backemeyer

PHOTOGRAPHIC CREDITS

Anthony Crickmay, Theatre Museum/V & A Picture Library
  47, 48, 49, 102, 103, 104
Vijay Dhir **10, 13, 14, 28-39, 66, 68-71**
Zoë Dominic **9**
Brian Tarr **81, 82**
Theatre Museum/V & A Picture Library **11, 12, 75, 79**
Nancy Yuen p.129

All other photographs by courtesy of Ralph Koltai

All quotations about the production by Ralph Koltai
unless otherwise stated

Title spread
Tales of Hoffman
Model photograph

CONTENTS

THE ROLE OF THE STAGE DESIGNER

'Despite a production being a collaborative effort, the designer is a very lonely animal.'

'Confronted by opinions expressed, advice given, criticism, sound and interesting ideas interspersed with half-baked and plain silly ones, the designer has to distinguish between them; know when to argue and when to keep quiet; and guard against praise, which can be very seductive and convenient but not necessarily justified. He has to create an envelope – provide an atmosphere – that serves the author, the director and focuses on the actor by letting him belong to the environment and the environment to him – *he* is the most important person of all. For the designer to succeed requires a pronounced critical faculty, for he must also remain true to himself as a creative artist. So that when I said the designer is very alone, it is that in the final analysis the decisions are his. It is entirely a matter of decisions. The quality and appropriateness of the design is dependent on these. Therein lies the difficulty – to recognise the right decision.'

Ralph Koltai
from *Theatre Design: The Exploration of Space*

FOREWORD

A century ago the Central School of Arts and Crafts first opened its doors to talented students wishing to develop their art practice. Over the ensuing years the College has grown in size, in the number of disciplines taught and has merged with Saint Martin's School of Art to become Central Saint Martins College of Art and Design. Currently occupying several sites in the heart of London, the College's physical presence is well established, yet its standing in the wider community rests on the achievements of past and present students and staff. It gives me great pleasure to be involved in celebrating the work of one of Central's most distinguished graduates and staff members, the theatre designer Ralph Koltai.

Ralph Koltai has been involved with Central Saint Martins College of Art and Design for over forty years, from student to teacher, to Head of the Theatre Design Department, and now consultant and Fellow of the London Institute. He has been instrumental in inspiring a generation of students, many now designers of international repute, making a significant contribution to Britain's pre-eminence in theatre design in the world.

As his own critical faculties developed he took his students with him along the road of discovery, from John Gunter, Sally Jacobs, Eileen Diss of the 1950s to Nadine Baylis, Terry Parsons and onwards to Sue Blane, Alison Chitty, Maria Bjornson and John Napier. He is constantly surprised and pleased to encounter ex-students in theatres across the globe from here to Australia.

In 1967, soon after the Jeanetta Cochrane Theatre was completed, Ralph linked the third-year theatre design students to choreographers and dancers of the Ballet Rambert in a series of original works entitled *Collaborations.* He followed that a year later in founding the London Traverse at the Jeanetta Cochrane Theatre with Jim Haynes, director of the Edinburgh Traverse, Charles Marowitz and Michael Geliot with the express intention of exposing his students to a professional work situation.

In his Introduction, Trevor Nunn, Director Emeritus of the Royal Shakespeare Company and past director of the Royal National Theatre, pays tribute to Ralph's impact in the development of theatre presentation internationally. Mike Barnett, Norman Morrice and John Napier, distinguished in their own fields, all reveal an innovative artist with the broadest vision and a deep concern for aesthetic values and technological advance.

Ralph Koltai is the recipient of many honours and awards attesting to his pre-eminence in the art of theatre design. In 1996 he became an Honorary Fellow of the London Institute and, whilst there can be no substitute for experiencing his work in the theatre, I hope this book will serve as a fitting tribute to his achievements. I would like to thank all those who have contributed to it.

Professor Margaret Buck
Head of College

INTRODUCTION

When asked to provide the setting for a play, the good designer doesn't try to produce an 'art object', complete, finished, and subject only to aesthetic laws. However beautiful in itself such a work might be, it is unlikely that it will require a play to be performed on it. The best theatre designs are incomplete without the actors, just as good theatre writing needs to be acted before it will come alive.

The theatre is a collective art, best undertaken in generous collaboration. Plays are illuminated and communicated by actors, directors and designers, but their work is individually incomplete, and entirely interdependent. So it is difficult to extract one element from a complex form, for assessment and evaluation. Critics are notoriously unable to distinguish between the actor's, the director's and the designer's contribution, and in a way, it is best so. Few people who work in the theatre are happy if their contribution is singled out as the only successful element in an otherwise unsatisfactory experience, because the collaborators all want the play to work above everything else; when the collective endeavour does become successful, the collaborators discover the intense and unique pleasure that derives from a group of people who have shared in a mystery.

Should the theatre remain a mystery? We live at a time when people demand to know more about everything; and because of television, newspapers and specialist magazines, the surprising thing is that mysteries, however much they are explained, rarely lose their power. Since the late 1970s there has been the opportunity to see and read a large number of documentary studies about how a play is rehearsed, directed, cast; reporters have looked into the backstage life of countless stage productions, films and television programmes in the making, but still audiences are able, under the influence of the play or the film itself, to suspend disbelief, forgetting that they know how it is all done.

The area that has received inadequate documentary attention is the work of the stage designer and this book, presenting the work of one the best stage designers in the world, is long overdue and much to be welcomed.

Ralph Koltai's curriculum vitae reads like a history of the developments of the last forty years of theatre in this country. He was one of the first contributors to the repertoire of the Royal Shakespeare Company. After the first few years of the company working in both Stratford and London, it became clear that a classical repertoire house with a permanent ensemble was as possible here as it had been for decades (if not centuries) before in the rest of Europe. With the formation of the RSC came the argument for state subsidy, and it is the subsidised theatre which has created conditions in which designers have been able to find continuity and security, which in turn prompted great daring and experiment in design solutions. Ralph Koltai's association with the RSC has been so successful that he has worked closely with the company for over twenty-five years.

Ralph has had a no less close and no less successful association with the National Theatre, and has helped to solve the problems created by the stages of these auditoria, The Olivier and The Lyttleton; in particular his breathtaking work on Ibsen's poetic masterpiece *Brand*, showed that the new stage could not be served by imaginative use of traditional thinking.

Significantly, to accompany the huge growth in theatre scale and output once the RSC and National were in full swing, there was a movement (which remains with us) towards small intimate theatre. Partly influenced by the development of the Fringe in the 1960s and partly because of ideas emanating from the big subsidised companies themselves, there was a concentration on one-room theatre, where the audience and actors share the same space.

Ralph Koltai was a leader in establishing the disciplines of small theatre production, relishing the challenge of working in primitive conditions with very small sums of money, in circumstances where invention is if not the mother, at least the brother of necessity. Two designs for The Other Place, the RSC's small theatre in Stratford, for *Baal* and *Sons of Light*, brilliantly demonstrate that small theatres with small resources need great talents.

Ralph Koltai's career has never been circumscribed by category or country. He is by nature a restless and questing spirit who has worked in many traditions throughout Europe and beyond. He has developed special relationships with companies and directors but he is always open to new influences, to the requirements of commercial theatre and above all to the challenge of the opera house. The examples in this volume of his opera designs are startling and provocative and make one yearn to see them all in operation in the opera house.

It is obvious from these photographs that Ralph Koltai has a very original sense of the use of materials and great interpretative boldness, but we appreciate his true worth if we feel that through this book he is leading us back to the theatre. I do hope, in the most stimulating way possible that after studying this superb book, you are like me thoroughly unsatisfied.

Trevor Nunn
Director Emeritus of the Royal Shakespeare Company

TWELFTH NIGHT
1996

'A landscape of hope
and fantasies of love.'

1
Production photograph

2
Production photograph

3
Production photograph

4
Model photograph

John Napier was one of Ralph Koltai's students while he was Head of Department of Theatre Design at Central School of Art and Design. His work includes many of the most successful and spectacular productions of the last two decades, including *Cats, Les Misérables, Miss Saigon* and *Starlight Express*. His admiration and respect for his mentor are unequivocal and he speaks passionately about their long-standing relationship.

'I owe my entire career to Ralph Koltai. He saw something in me I couldn't see myself. In the mid-sixties I applied for a place on the design course at the Central School of Art and Design and in the first year Ralph was one of several tutors I had some contact with. He was fascinated by my background – I'd trained in sculpture – and the fact that I would spend time melting down lead and take hours beating it around. Nowadays these processes are taken for granted but then theatre design was essentially French flats [traditional scenery]. Ralph and John Bury were the first people to use different materials like scaffolding, real wood and cement, but this sensibility had not spread through the department at the time and I decided to leave at the end of the first year because the course was old-fashioned and lacked weight. I was perplexed, coming from the discipline of sculpture which seemed to be trying to break barriers and ask fundamental philosophical questions, to be met with a form set in aspic which seemed to attract those more interested in decoration.

While I was trying to make my way outside college I got a telephone call; it was Ralph Koltai saying that he had become Head of Department and would I please come back and continue the course. He felt that I was one of the students who showed promise and was likely to influence the work that was being done there. I knew from my earlier encounters with Ralph that he was a tough disciplinarian and also interested in abstract forms, and I agreed to go back. In the second year my work really seemed to flourish under Ralph. He allowed me to use my imagination to develop things that maybe were imbecilic or crazy but at least they were testing ideas. I didn't go to Central to acquire received ideas but to discover what it was that needed to be done. He understood that this was a process you had to go through in order to make any sort of change. Ralph saw that I was different but still capable of doing something and doing it in a fundamentally different way that would be valued in the modern world. He was not only a great mentor, he also encouraged us to go and see things in the theatre, to experience the work of Svoboda and the World Theatre season, for example. Because he was a working designer and not simply teaching, he was constantly in contact with the theatre world. He started the whole process of collaboration between students and working directors. He would cajole people at the National and the Opera House to come in and work with us, which was of immense benefit.

During my second year something bizarre happened. As I recall there was some form of celebration at the Central School and, as a result, rather than having a graduate exhibition of third-year work they mounted a show in which all years took part. The Theatre Design Department took over most of the main exhibition halls and I had two or three models displayed – *Tamburlaine*, *Oedipus Rex* and a Brecht piece, I believe. Many in the theatre community came to see the exhibition, including John Hales, who had just taken over the Phoenix Theatre in Leicester. On the spot he offered me the job of Head of Design at the Phoenix. It was a huge dilemma; on the one hand I would be insane not to take the job, but on the other hand I also had an allegiance to Ralph. I was one of the people who had really bonded with him and I felt I owed him something. He was responsible for starting a fundamental rethink of attitudes towards theatre design and I was part of it. Finally I decided to take the job but to carry on at the Central and to use my professional practice as my diploma work. I didn't actually sit a lot of the exam work although I did pass and somewhere deep in the bowels of the Central lies a diploma that I have yet to receive!

I had to resign from Leicester after eighteen months because the director who had given me the job resigned. I came back down to London with a young family and no prospects whatsoever. I was working in a factory trying to support myself and my family when out of the blue came this request from someone wishing to see me. It turned out to be the director Charles Marowitz, who was doing a production of Peter Barnes' play *The Ruling Class* in Nottingham, and Ralph was originally going to be designing the work. For some reason he couldn't do the show and the person he recommended to take on the job was me. It must have taken a huge leap of imagination to recommend this out-of-work ex-student. I met Charles Marowitz and he gave me the job. It was about to be put on when a dispute concerning an actor resulted in Marowitz leaving the project. Fortunately Stuart Burge took on the production and it became a huge success, both in Nottingham and subsequently in London.

After this, Ralph still kept an eye on me, encouraged me, and came to see the work that I was doing. I think he was quite proud of me and we've kept in touch. I owe him a spectacular amount and the sense of gratitude I have is such that there is nothing I would not do for him. He is my mentor and my father-figure in terms of the art world. His enthusiasm, his knowledge, his talent and the analytical ability of his mind, his courage and his fantastic skill as a raconteur – these are all things I value

in him. In many ways Ralph is the father of modern British theatre design, possibly alongside John Bury and Tim O'Brien, though I would have to put him above those two because of the bond I have with him.

I think Ralph would have made a great painter but he chose the form of theatre design as his art and he has pursued that. Ralph has the capacity to do things that are vibrant, sensual, wonderfully observed and sexy. It doesn't always work, but when it does it is sensational. Ralph will find brilliant solutions to problems and come up with amazing ideas yet he never tries to set a style.

I'm a little tired of hearing about "designer's theatre" and how people like Ralph and me are mechanising the stage. It seems absurd considering there was machinery in the theatre in the Jacobean age and the succeeding centuries and I suspect it was far greater than anything we would do today. Some people will not accept that we are living in the twentieth century and have moved on from the quill pen, even the typewriter. We are now in the age of desktop publishing and Windows, the tools that journalists use to write their reviews, yet when Ralph and I use a piece of machinery on stage we are regarded as philistines for departing from bare boards and the actor's voice. These things are fine for certain productions but shouldn't be clung to at all costs. The thing is that when these disparate elements come together that's when you get the great productions, like Ralph's *As You Like It* or *Nicholas Nickleby* – it comes down to invention and the result of one thing feeding off another. Anyway, Ralph taught me how to use all that "mechanical stuff" so I'll blame him!

The thing that Ralph understood which nobody else understood and which is something he and I are in complete agreement about is that pure design is about the manipulation of abstract objects in a space in order to give that space an atmosphere or mood that enhances the nature of what's happening in that space. It's not about pictorial representation but about placing things in such a way that the audience will believe in what is going on. Neither of us are remotely interested in re-inventing "scenery".'

TAVERNER
1972

'A power struggle between Church and Monarchy. A composite image of the cross, the sword and the balance.'

5
Production photograph

6
Model photograph

7
Production photograph

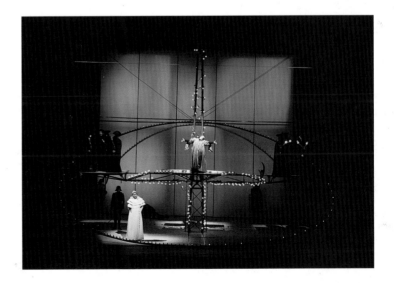

8
Production photograph

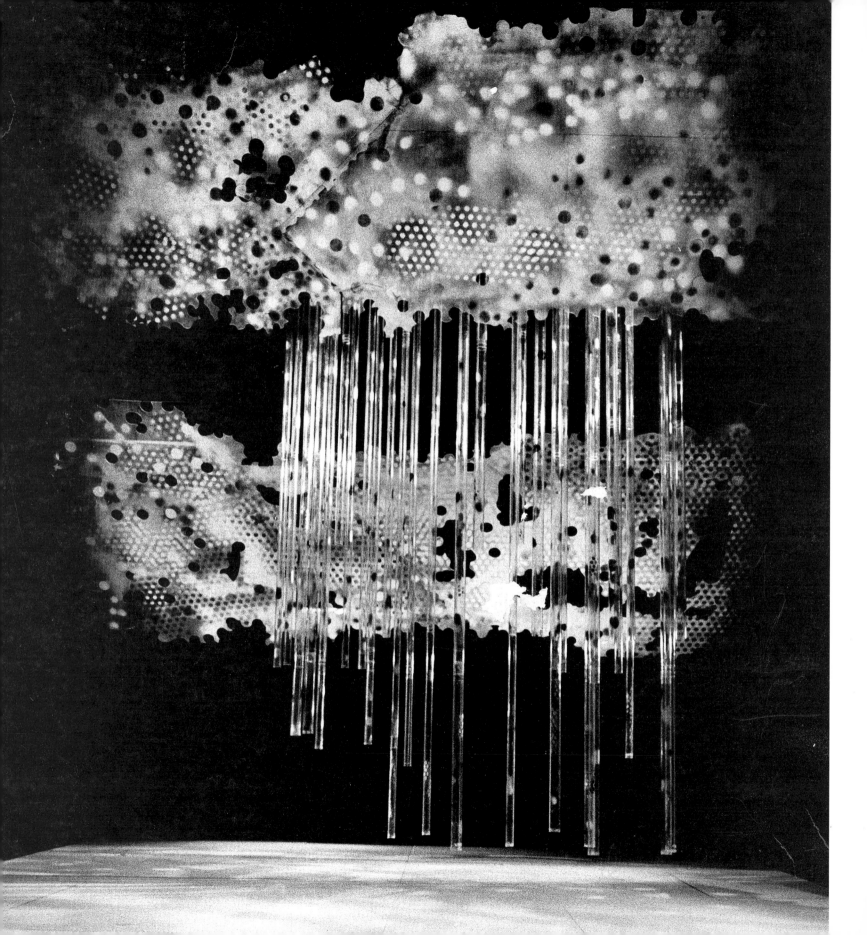

AS YOU LIKE IT
1967

'The Forest of Arden is real to those who dream it.'

9
Production photograph

10
Orlando

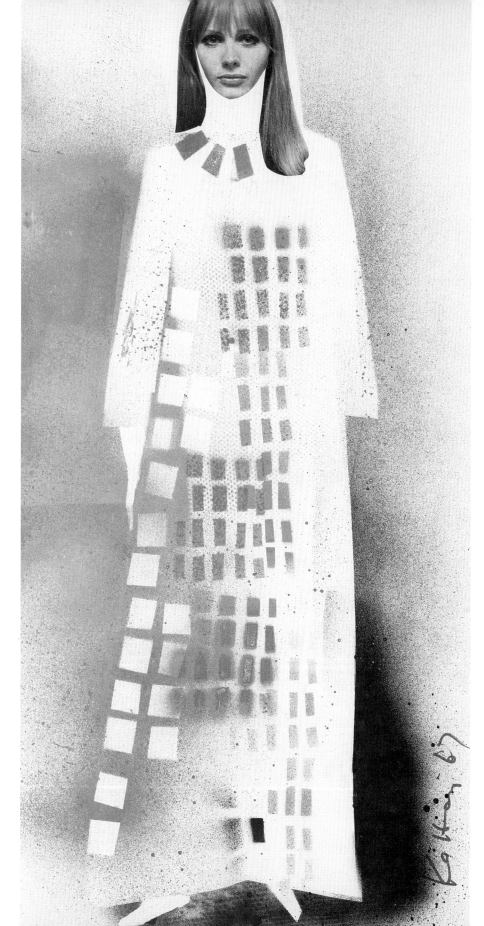

11
Rosalind

12
Celia

13
Jacques

14
Touchstone

pages 22-23
15
Cosmic Prologue
Model photograph

16
Mercury
Model photograph

THE PLANETS
1990

17
Venus
Model photograph

18
Mars
Model photograph

19
Jupiter
Model photograph

20
Saturn
Model photograph

OTHELLO
1985

'An exercise in kinetic art with a peripheral hint at sexuality.'

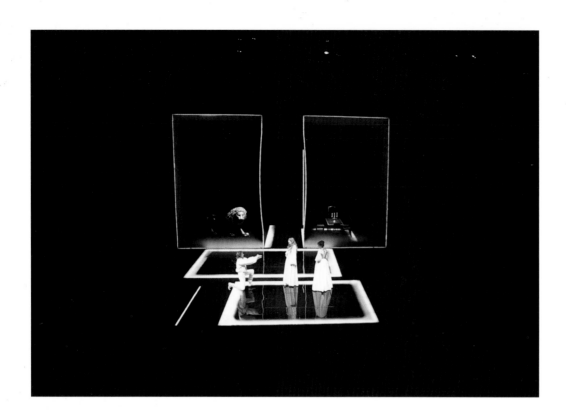

21
Production photograph

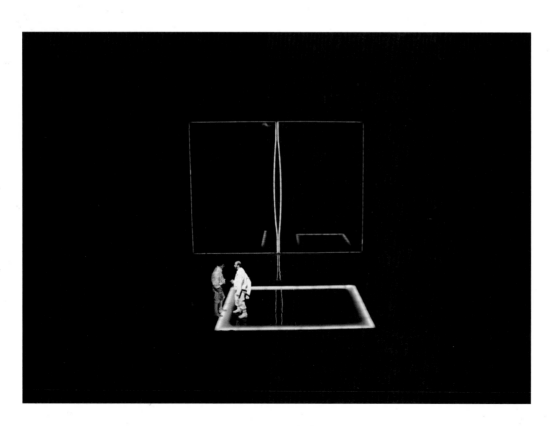

22
Production photograph

25
Set with projection
Production photograph

pages 28-29
24
Basic set for *Baal*
Model photograph

'Three sails of the ghost-
ship rising from the sea.'

26
Production photograph

MADAM BUTTERFLY
1995

'An idealised vision of Japan through American (Pinkerton's) eyes.'

27
Model photograph

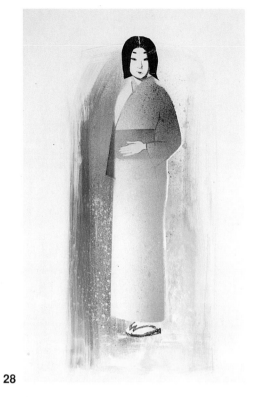

28

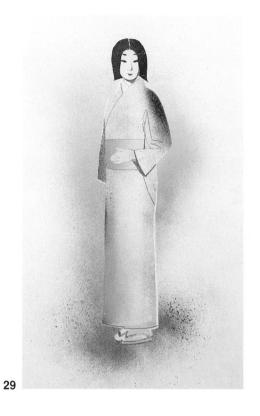

29

30

Geisha costumes

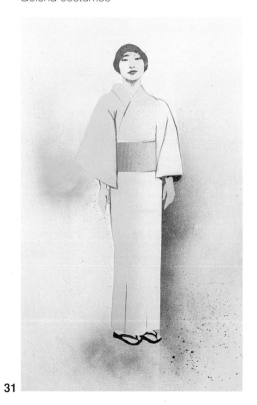

31

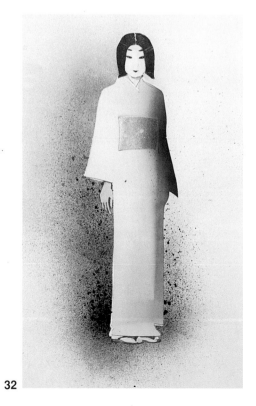

32

33

34

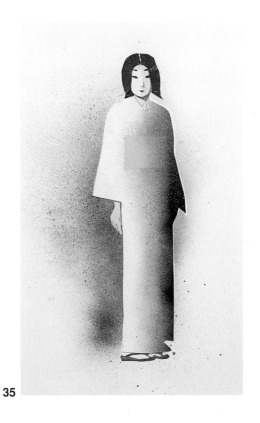

35

36

37

38

39

A MIDSUMMER MARRIAGE
1976

'A fantasy world of magic, legend and mysticism.'

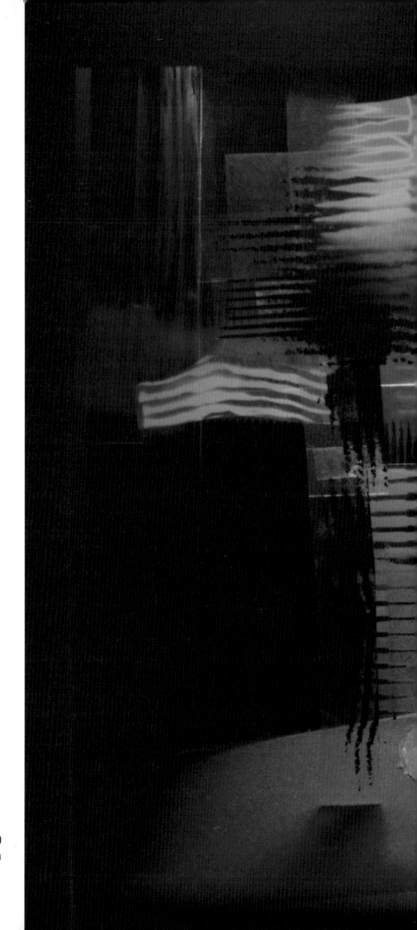

40
Model photograph

'The mirrored floor and walls reflecting the narcissistic nature of the characters.'

42
Model photograph

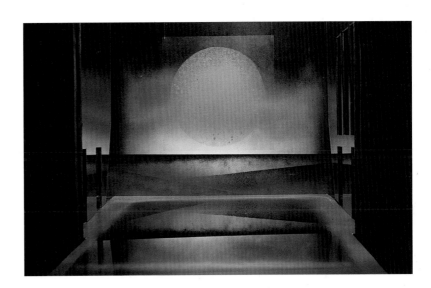

41
Model photograph

43
Model photograph

THE MAKROPULOS AFFAIR
1991

'Inspired by the catacombs along the Appian Way.'

45
Production photograph

44
Model photograph

'A world in cosmic space.
Coincided with the first Apollo landing on the moon.'

47
The Rhinegold
Model photograph

46
Valkyrie and *Siegfried*, Act III
Model photograph

left
48
Brunhilde's Cave
Model photograph

49
Wotan, the Valkyrie
Production photograph

CUL DE SAC
1964

'A narrative ballet – a building site. The paper screen torn from the hoarding makes fantasy of reality.'

49
Basic set
Model photograph

NORMAN MORRICE   talking to Tim White

Norman Morrice is one of the key figures in the development of dance in Britain. Following a long involvement with Ballet Rambert, as dancer, choreographer, associate director and co-director, he was Artistic Director of the Royal Ballet from 1977 to 1986. He has taught throughout the world and is currently Director of Choreographic Studies at the Royal Ballet School. Ralph Koltai's first experience of designing for dance coincided with Norman Morrice's choreographic debut. An enthusiastic dancer with Ballet Rambert since 1952, Norman Morrice was encouraged to create his own work by Madame Rambert. The manager of the company, Fred Bromwich, had persuaded Madame Rambert to visit an exhibition of Ralph Koltai's work, on the strength of which a meeting was arranged between Morrice and the young designer.

'We hit it off immediately. I had no idea what to do about designing my very first ballet. At that time we had no such thing as composition classes so that everything you learnt was from watching other people's work and this also applied to design, which you saw in an Ashton work or a Balanchine work or whatever. There were a few designers associated with Rambert whose works were in the repertory, Sophie Fedorovitch and Hugh Stevenson for example, and so one learned from these how a design worked in practice. Being a dancer myself, however, meant that I never saw anything from out front.

When I talked to Ralph about the possibilities of working together on this first piece he really opened my eyes to colour, shape, texture and how you could best serve the choreography and the music as a composite. I got excited. He made me look at buildings, made me look *up*, instead of just down at the pavement. He was mad for taking photographs all the time and always had masses of pictures of things like doors used to block up bombed-out buildings. He did a whole series of what to me looked like paintings but were simply what was there – peeling paint on a blue door and next to it a door with scribbling on it. He would take something like that and use it to link up with what we were talking about and suggest further ideas for the choreography. The moment I started describing what I thought I wanted, Ralph would verbalise ideas. Out of this dialogue *Two Brothers* evolved into a slightly desolate, edge-of-town location, where young people might meet. The story was based on the James Dean film *East of Eden* and from this Ralph described what the location might be. He wanted to create something strong dramatically and settled on a wall that came out at an angle toward the audience, increasing in size. Ralph raised the question of how the youths got to this space, hence the bicycle. The sense of this being a forgotten area was heightened by a ladder and hanging tarpaulins. There was a totally abstract background which I didn't think was real when I first saw it. Of course, by the time the set was complete, it was exactly right.

As we didn't have a lighting rig – this was the old Rambert – he decided to get a telegraph pole with a 'practical' – a bare bulb – coming out of it. It was a very dramatic moment when, as twilight disappeared, the bulb came on. I was very excited by this, even knowing that the telegraph pole was a canvas thing held down at the bottom with a stage weight! There wasn't a lot of money around and *Two Brothers* had a very inexpensive set. Ralph's ambition very rapidly expanded after we'd had our first success and his sets became more and more difficult and expensive to realise. The one that almost caused a total riot was for a piece called *The Travellers*. There was a lot of metal – metal wings that revolved, a huge back wall, an expanded steel staircase and roller shutter doors – which of course had to tour. Crews around the country were not used to handling great sheets of metal which entailed wearing special protective clothing.

In most of the work we created there was a sense of transition. Both of us were very concerned about the things going on around us. *A Place in the Desert* centred around the Aswan Dam which was being built in the background. It was there the whole time but you couldn't see it at the beginning. Gradually you became aware that the entire village was going to be under water in a very short time and that everybody had to leave. All of the works had a particular theme and we didn't do anything approaching what people would call "abstract" until we got to *Conflicts*. This piece came about very much as a result of having been to America and seen the developments in modern dance over there. I came back to tell Ralph about all these amazing kinds of moving that we didn't know about. We both knew we had to do something very different and what we created *was* very different. For *Conflicts*, Ralph took photographs of the company and distorted them. Large glass slides were made so they could be projected. We operated on an empty stage and backstage area in which everything was exposed. This was one of the first times in dance where the stage was opened up in this way to make the stage machinery visible. All that remained on the stage was a half canvas cloth that could have been there to be painted, on which the slides were projected. There was only one "practical" item, which was a chair.

There was a very close relationship between the design and the choreography in our works. When we were creating *Hazaña*, Ralph got all the clothes from a second-hand market. The dancers loved this because it made them feel absolutely right for the piece, which centres around the action of one man carrying a cross up wooden scaffolding on a church wall, a cross that was weighed down to the point where the dancer had to exert real effort to accomplish the task. This close relationship was very much a reflection of the relationship that existed between Ralph and the company – because he was so easy to get on with, everybody talked to him and he talked to them. He was also an influence on the company, coming from the world of art and design. Because of Ralph one would go and see a particular exhibition; he was very good at communicating his enthusiasm to the entire cast. Prior to this a dancer would never have any communication with the designer – it had always been "this is your costume". You might have seen a bit of paper with your costume on it, you had a fitting and that was it. The dancer didn't connect this process with the choreography; the design was simply another thing that somebody else handled. Ralph turned the design process into a living thing that evolved on a daily basis and involved all of us in the company. Because the dancers were so integral to the creative process, they were feeding both Ralph and me with their ideas. The relationships between the members of the company became the subject matter of *Conflicts*. I was dying to bring on a character that would be Ralph Koltai but I didn't dare!

Ralph was part of the change that took place in the Rambert company in 1966 when it went from a medium-size organisation touring pocket versions of the classics to a small ensemble committed to contemporary work. Prior to this, Ralph and I had produced a presentation about the possibility of a dance theatre that the Mercury Trust was hoping to establish in Notting Hill Gate. Ralph's position as Head of the Theatre Design Department at Central and the availability of the Jeannetta Cochrane Theatre coincided with the need for change at Rambert. Some people thought the dance company was on its last legs, going to a tiny little unknown theatre, but I think we proved them wrong within a couple of years and gave courage to others. From the outset we had intended to mount a series of collaborations between the dance company and the students on the theatre design course. These programmes gave opportunities for designers such as Nadine Baylis and John Napier.

 I was spoilt by working with Ralph, having such a rewarding relationship with a designer. I learnt that the work could only be done if the designer's influence was as great as mine. Ralph had to be part of the essential creation before he could begin to think of models or costumes on paper. He instilled in me a concern to move the art forward and to discover things in the process of creating the work. Talking to other designers who were involved with the company I was aware that the relationship between Ralph and me was very special. I hope we were able to generate similar relationships between the choreographers and designers we brought together.'

TWO BROTHERS
1958

50
Set design drawing

BRAND
1978

'A Nordic frozen landscape.'

52
Model photograph

51
Production photograph

53
Production photograph

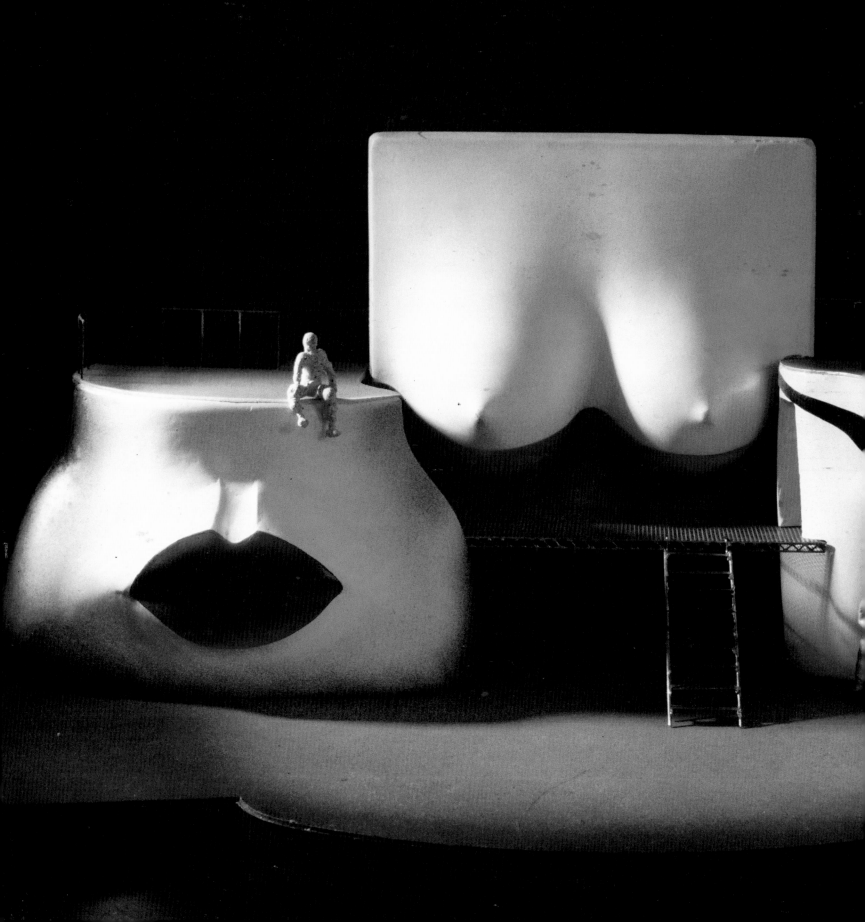

DIE SOLDATEN
1983

'I need four acting areas.' Ken Russell (Director)

54
Model photograph

55
Production photograph

56
Production photograph

57
Production photograph

CYRANO DE BERGERAC
1984

'Act V – A Convent Garden. The autumn of Cyrano's life: the crown of a tree shedding its leaves, hinting at stained glass, a rose window …'

59
Production photograph

58
Model photograph

61
Production photograph

60
Production photograph

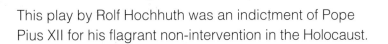

THE REPRESENTATIVE
1963

This play by Rolf Hochhuth was an indictment of Pope Pius XII for his flagrant non-intervention in the Holocaust.

As a survivor of the 'Final Solution', and later a member of the British Delegation to the International Military Tribunal, Nuremberg, and War Crimes Interrogation Unit from 1945 to 1948, this play has a deep personal significance for me. I could see no way of making any visual statement to encompass the event, the murder of six million Jews. Weeks passed in hours of talks with Robert David Macdonald, Hochhuth's translator, on moral questions and facts known to us both. During that period a 'design solution' was secondary and not under discussion. The play contains scenes set in various locations from a beer cellar in Berlin to an ante-chamber in the Vatican and a final scene at Auschwitz. No crematoria, no gas chamber. Yet the essence of the play was exactly that and became my metaphor and eventual solution. All scenes were set within that obscene, anonymous concrete chamber.

Ralph Koltai

62
The Pope's ante-chamber
Model photograph

THE TEMPEST
1978

'An island of the mind.'

63
Model photograph

OEDIPUS TYRANNUS
1974

'I want a sexual landscape.' Hovhanness I Pilikian (Director)

64
Model photograph

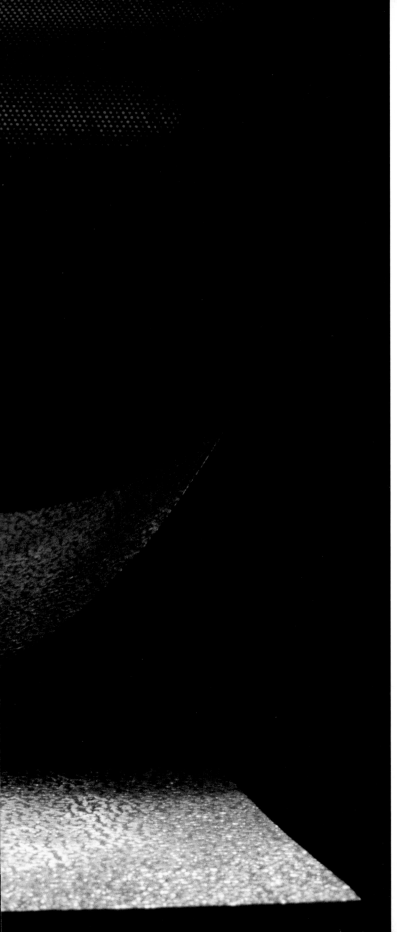

TERRA NOVA
1981

'Stainless steel – abstracted polar ice-scape.'

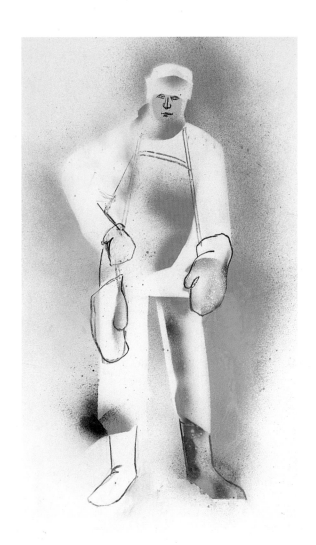

66
Scott

65
Model photograph

67
Production photograph

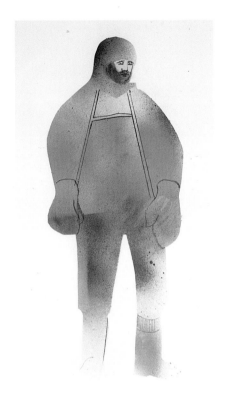

68
Oates

69
Evans

70
Wilson

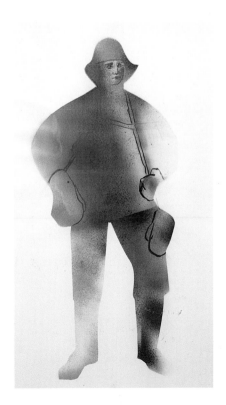

71
Bowers

72
Overture
Model photograph

73
Model photograph

74
Production photograph

75
Male worker
Costume design

76
Production photograph

77
Production photograph

78
Maria
Costume design

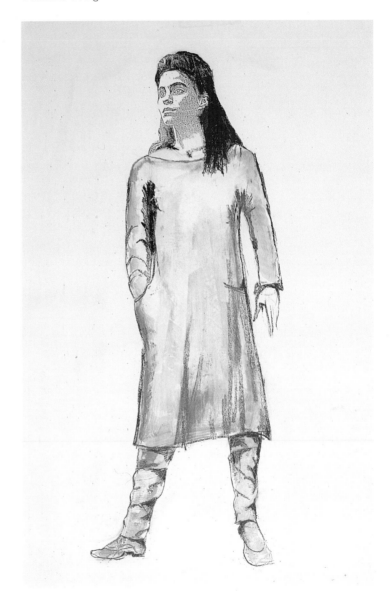

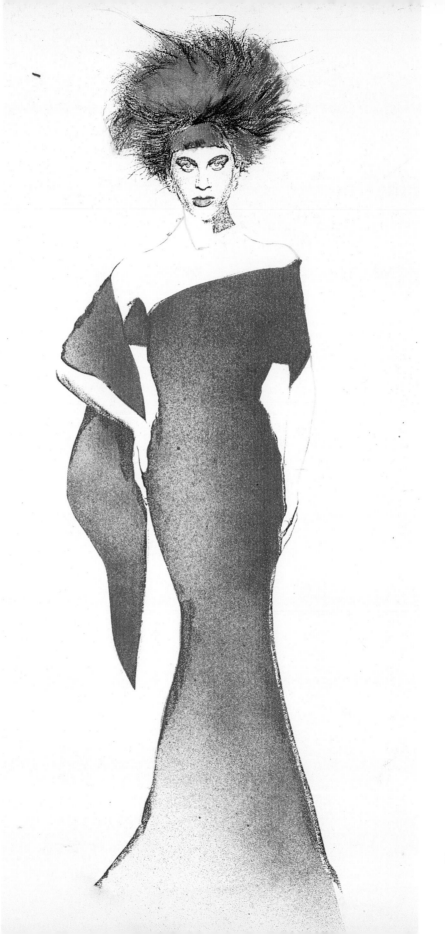

79
Futura
Costume design

80
Production photograph

78

MIKE BARNETT   talking to Tim White

A chartered mechanical engineer, Mike Barnett works as a freelance design engineer, realising some of the most imaginative and complex environments created for the stage. He first worked with Ralph Koltai on *Brand* in 1978 and has most recently collaborated with him on the 1997 Welsh National Opera production of *Simon Boccanegra*.

'I first met Ralph in 1978 when he was designing Ibsen's *Brand*. *Brand* was one of the early productions at the National in the Olivier Theatre. *Brand* was a big set and a lot of the time was spent dealing with the handling and weight-problems which represented the side of a mountain with various traps and access points. The mountain was covered in snow at the higher levels, gradually changing to green in the lower acting areas. The piece ended with an avalanche, during which all sections moved rapidly. When a big show is planned it is usually known sometime in advance that there will be certain problems that need to be solved, and so at an early stage I would discuss with Ralph the feasibility of what he wanted to do. Even with a cardboard 1:25 model it is possible to discover what will be problematic and often things that appear difficult are quite easy to achieve.

Ralph claims that he doesn't have any idea about engineering, but he is actually an intuitive engineer. He sees reality; he is able to see what is feasible and what is not. With a set by Ralph you'll know that what he's designed is possible and the problem then lies with the usual budgetary constraints. For example, every time a large musical goes on, there are always stringent limitations on money, although it might not seem the case in some instances. To economise you have to work closely with the designer because when the cost of the setting has exceeded the budget you need to know where you can save money without being destructive to the idea.

What Ralph brings to me ends up being pretty close to the design that gets to the stage. An example of this was *Metropolis*. I remember when Ralph presented the model to the production team the room went very quiet. Ralph was happily demonstrating – "this goes up here" and "this comes down and that moves across there" – and looking around the room I realised we were all trying to imagine how many millions it was going to cost!

One of the highlights of the set were giant machine units made from moulded fibreglass weighing several tons. They floated on airpads because they had to travel over a relatively thin illuminated plexiglass floor that would not have been strong enough to support anything on wheels. There were six pads to each unit which operated rather like a hovercraft and any small gap in the stage floor would cause them to deflate. I remember spending the previews armed with a bicycle puncture repair kit to keep the pads afloat!

At the sides of the set and centre stage were traps for elevators to travel through – the overall effect was very close to the 1926 Fritz Lang film. The complex plot was based on the notion that below the city of Metropolis workers maintain giant machines to support the élitists who live above ground. Early on in the story, Maria, spiritual leader of the workers, makes a bid for a moment of freedom and takes some children to the surface to see the sun. For this scene we had an effect nicknamed "the grassy knoll". Suspended on the back wall, and concealed by abstract illuminated projections, was an articulated floor that slid, caterpillar-like over the existing floor of the stage. The new covering, representing the outside world, was lush green grass, a stunning contrast to the grey and black uniformity of the mechanical world. Through the middle of this new floor, a capsule rose bearing the cast. There was only a two-inch allowance for the elevator to get through the hole.

Another key effect was used in the ballroom scene. It is here that Futura, the robot invented by John Freeman, master of Metropolis, makes her first appearance. Ralph wanted a suitably grand entrance so he decided to lower her through the mirrored ballroom ceiling which was angled against the back edge of the floor rising to the top of the proscenium at the front of the stage. Again the tolerance around the space in the ceiling was very small and the slightest vibration or breeze would send the line off course. We devised a lowering system that worked so quickly that by the time the audience realised what was happening, the door of Futura's capsule had slid open and she had stepped out.

Ralph is acquisitive – you have to watch science and technology because there is always something you can use or some spin-off that can assist in what you are trying to do. In *Simon Boccanegra* for the Welsh National Opera, which is a touring production, Ralph's concept consists of two complicated suspended tracks which are a 'V' form in plan, on each of which is suspended a travelling wall that rotates so that both sides are visible. One wall is made of clear plexiglass, partially silvered and lit to look airily transparent, with an open doorway. The opposite wall appears as an enormously complex piece of rusty steel. Ralph found a rusted piece of farm equipment at his home in France and he was fascinated with the texture. He took the material to the local blacksmith to cut a gash into it with an acetylene torch.

We realised that for technical considerations it had to be made of fibreglass and in several sections to enable it to tour. It weighed about three-quarters of a ton and the combined weight of the two walls and track came to around two tons.

Ralph prefers to create his designs three-dimensionally and I'm sure he loves nothing more than to be in an engineering workshop with the problem right in front of him.'

SIMON BOCCANEGRA
1997

'The collision of two worlds – Patricians versus Plebeians.'

81
Model photograph

82
Model photograph

84
Production photograph

85
Production photograph

83
Production photograph

TANNHÄUSER

Geneva Opera
1986

86
Model photograph

87
Model photograph

88
Production photograph

89
Production photograph

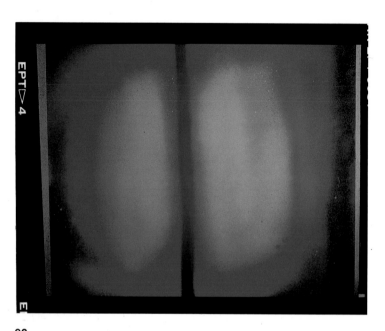

90

Venusberg projections

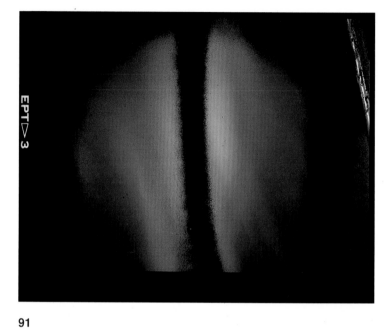

91

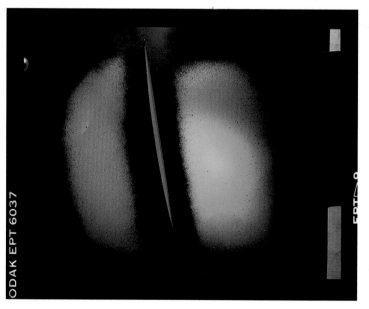

92

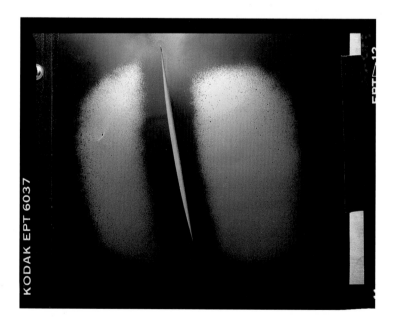

93

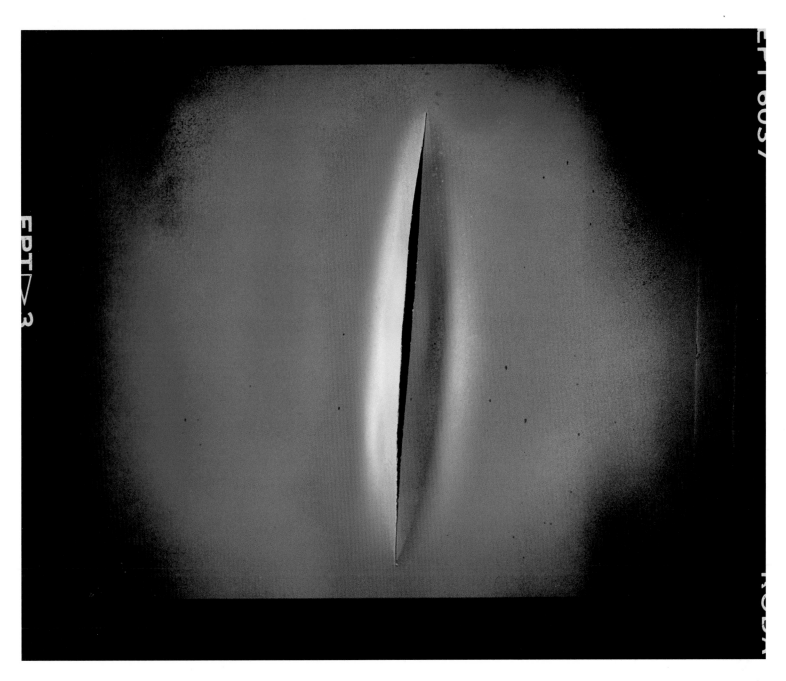

94

TANNHÄUSER
Sydney Opera
1973

95
Model photograph

THE HOUSE OF BERNARDA ALBA
1996

CARMEN
1997

'Blood, heat and sexual jealousy. Design takes advantage of the height of the Albert Hall, London.'

98
Model photograph

99
Production photograph

THE JEW
OF MALTA
1964

100
Production photograph

101
Model photograph

BACK TO METHUSELAH
1969

'A cosmic prologue, transformation into the Garden of Eden and the Tree of Knowledge.'

103
Production photograph

102
Production photograph

104
Production photograph

A DISTINCTIVE VISION

Ralph Koltai's distinguished career which covers a period of nearly fifty years continues to astonish and to provoke new ways of looking at well-known classic works, as a result of his strong personal aesthetic. From the first collaboration with the Ballet Rambert created with the choreographer Norman Morrice, through to the huge variety of drama work with national companies, operas, ballets, and musicals, Koltai is renowned both as a designer and a director in many countries. To date he has created over 200 productions on the stage vividly demonstrating his unique ability to respond to the demands of the individual commission while maintaining a clear and individual personal voice that is unmistakably Ralph Koltai.

Koltai was a 'scenographer' in Great Britain before the word 'scenography' – the total creation of the stage including the visual direction of the performers – was in general use. Koltai has a unique and often oblique view of reality, never settling for the obvious. He often uses startling opposing images, that are utterly appropriate and breathtakingly daring. The huge concrete wall that confronted the audience for Rolf Hochhuth's *The Representative* slid slowly open to reveal the Pope holding court in a gas chamber. In this image he showed the unspeakable, finding a definitive statement for the Holocaust. This production was a significant artistic and personal statement for Koltai, informing the entire understanding of the play. The last scene, which was set in Auschwitz, was described only with lines of barbed wire. Bamber Gascoigne in his review in *The Observer*, 29 September 1963, notes that 'Ralph Koltai has designed the sets with stark effect; in fact the image of the barbed wire in the last scene … appears

to be Koltai's rather than Hochhuth's'. This mixture of fact and fiction, art and metaphor, investigating different forms of reality, is the essence of the scenographer's art. The exhibits show above all Koltai's instinctive ability to translate a vast emotional subject into a simple abstract image, that lives in the imaginary world of the theatre.

His early training as a graphic artist at Epsom School of Art in 1943 is demonstrated in the way that he manipulates shapes and objects in the stage space, that in themselves create a total composition of form, colour and textures. In particular there are striking portrayals of landscapes where the spectator's eye is taken to every plane of the stage space in a thrilling exploration of two-dimensional texture and colour in a three-dimensional sculptural space.

Many dramatists from Shakespeare to Ibsen have used nature as a stage metaphor for the human condition. Anton Chekhov in *The Seagull* describes the conflict between art and realism in trying to portray nature, which, in theatre terms, will always be no more than a poor imitation of reality. Ralph Koltai's approach is to recreate nature as an individual art form, similar to the approach of other contemporary photographers and environmental artists. He creates his own landscapes, using clean strong lines, contrasting reflective surfaces and a strong, bold use of colour – in fact, recreating nature. These 'recreated' landscapes, *Terra Nova, As You Like It, Brand, Twelfth Night, Much Ado About Nothing, Oedipus Tyrannus* often incorporate industrial and engineering techniques, combined with a daring use of new materials that enable the scenic movement within the space to reflect the human condition portrayed by the actors.

The reproductions in this volume demonstrate his masterly use of the stage space, but they can never convey the true feeling of an actual production, enlivened with actors, costumes and lights that are the primary elements of Koltai's art. Maquettes can be transformed into works of art in their own right, but when they are animated on the stage, they become living emotional spaces. This is well demonstrated in the operatic works where the statements of space always have a further dimension achieved by constantly re-inventing the stage space with moving elements during the progression of the opera. Large abstract stage statements are drawn into the particular needs of the scenes by moving the scenic elements in and out of the audience's focus, often constructed from dramatically contrasting materials. Koltai frequently uses found objects for the maquettes (in *Metropolis, Simon Boccanegra, The Representative* for example) such as parts of motor engines, rusty metal, farm utensils and concrete blocks, and by selecting parts of them, changes and enlarges the scale. These are reproduced twenty-five times larger for the actual stage production, always under Koltai's scrupulous and rigorous personal supervision.

He has collected a team of dedicated interpreters of his work, always generously welcoming their contribution to his aesthetic vision. Koltai has experimented with engineering techniques in collaboration with Mike Barnett, an engineer, and with many forms of plastics, perspex and polycarbonates with Charles Woolff, a pioneer in plastics technology. The ability to use these industrial materials in a theatre has become a distinctive Koltai signature. However, Koltai is not interested in exploring techniques for their own sake, although he is endlessly fascinated by technology. It all has to contribute to the central purpose – the experience of the spectator. The frequent use of mirrors and reflective surfaces allows the spectator to see further than the characters' own presentation of their roles, and to glimpse the consequences of action while the action is being performed. In this way, as Brecht has stated, we never forget we are in a theatre, a world into which we are transported for a moment of dramatic, and not real time. Koltai's strict aesthetic sense, informs the decisions of choice that are fundamental to the scenographer's art. He loves the hunt for the elusive key to the work in hand, the hunt, the chase, the kill when the final solution is consolidated into a concrete form. He often works with amazing speed, demonstrating that it is not the length of time in which the result is achieved that is its virtue, but the vision that encapsulates the feeling of the piece in its totality. This work is frequently done when he is seized by the need to turn the vision in his head into a maquette immediately in the loneliness of a long day's journey into night. Sometimes in the cool light of day he looks at his work and simply turns it the other way up and it is complete.

Ralph Koltai has said of himself that he 'gives directors what they want without them even knowing it'. In many instances he has probably directed the show as well as designed it. In this respect he has redefined the traditional role of the designer in the modern theatre, being amongst the first to insist that the designer was not here to draw up the director's idea, but to contribute to the whole concept of the production, providing an entire visual world that will throw a new light on a play or opera. His passion is to find that seminal visual idea that enables a piece of work to be totally expressed in the theatre space. In *Mahagonny* by Brecht and Weill, Koltai 'dreamed' an entire production and recorded it through a series of drawings and notes in an *Arbeitsbuch* which he showed to Lotte Lenya, Weill's widow, when he took her for English tea at Brown's Hotel at their first meeting. More than two years later, through her enthusiasm for his ideas the production took place at Sadler's Wells theatre. The astonished audience saw a completely bare stage, and a real battered truck and trailer drive on. The sides of the trailer were let down and became the stage for the City of Mahagonny. It was the first time Brecht was shown in England in a non-imitative manner, yet every image was politically appropriate and aesthetically thrilling.

Ralph Koltai started as a student in the Theatre Design Department at the Central School of Arts and Crafts, admitted after an interview with the painter Morris Kestleman, then Head of Fine Art, and went on to become Head of Department of Theatre Design. He encouraged, inspired and was a role model for a generation of great designers including John Napier, Maria Bjornson, Alison Chitty and many more. Ralph Koltai has given unstintingly and generously to young theatre designers just starting out on their careers, never failing to go to Degree Shows, and to seek out and speak to the exhibitors professionally, practically, and amusingly about their work, and the reality of the professional mine-field that lies ahead. Koltai was a founder, along with his contemporaries, John Bury, Timothy O'Brien and Nicholas Georgiadis, of the first professional association for theatre designers that was to become the Society of British Theatre Designers. He pioneered the now-accepted use of a contract for theatre designers, achieved representation for theatre designers by the British Actors Equity Association, and a schedule of conditions of work, which have now become established practice. He used his position of seniority to be publicly controversial, knowing this would not benefit him, but would be a voice for younger and less-represented members of the profession. In this context Ralph Koltai used his strategic skill acquired with British Army Intelligence, to publicly declare at a crowded embryonic meeting of the society all the fees he had been paid for his design work in the past few years. This act of cunning and bravery broke the stranglehold of silence that had permitted the pernicious practice of undercutting designers' fees. This contributed to Koltai's never-ending quest – to raise the public profile of theatre design. It is relatively rare nowadays for a designer not to be acknowledged in a review, yet too frequently, as he wryly observes, productions are still thought to be the total domain of the director.

This book enables us to see examples of Koltai's art from Japan, Hong Kong, Denmark and Norway as well as work conserved in private collections in Great Britain and Texas. The collection has been selected by the artist and reflects his uncompromising view of his work.

Pamela Howard, Scenographer
Curator, *Ralph Koltai, Theatre Designs
– The Exploration of Space*, The Lethaby Galleries,
28 October – 24 November 1997

THE RISE AND FALL OF THE CITY OF MAHAGONNY
1963

The one labour of love with no equal in my career. I came across the first post-war recording by Philips in Amsterdam in 1960. Captivated by Kurt Weill's score and Bertolt Brecht's book I conceived a production in the manner of a Brecht *Arbeitsbuch* with no expectation of its realisation. However, good fortune allowed me to make contact in New York with Lotte Lenya, widow of Weill, who played Jenny in the original 1928 production. She was the holder of the rights of her late husband's music. I contrived a very English meeting over tea at London's Brown's Hotel. Initially unenthusiastically resigned to meeting me (having been constantly pursued by requests for the performance rights), she gradually warmed to my ideas – not without criticism – as she turned the pages of my 'picture book'.

It took another three years for my dream to become a reality, when personally acting as consultant, she gave the rights to Sadler's Wells Opera, with the proviso that the opera be directed by Michael Geliot to my designs.

However the story does not end there. The rights to Brecht's book were held by his son, Stefan, who lived in Paris and hated his father. As with Lenya, I received a distinctly cool reception upon visiting his apartment overlooking the Seine. For some reason our conversation turned to photography and problems he was having with his camera. Somehow I fixed it, how I don't know, but I got the rights to the book.

Ralph Koltai

pages 106-120
105-119
Storyboard drawings

I

1.

Empty Stage - Cyclorama

2 permanent booms L and R with one loudspeaker
on each.

Opening light fairly dark- beams of headlamps
appear by projection on cyc.
Subsequently two beams cut across stage from
O.P. side

Head lamp proj. film

No. 1 contd.

Lorry is driven on stage, comes to rest Centre.

FATTY on tailboard

MOSES driving

BEGBICK behind tarpaulin on trailer.

Projection: —'WANTED' notices

No. 2.

Remove cabin of lorry during opening
announcement :'Rasch wuchs in den ......'

Flap side of lorry down to cover wheels.

Strike pile of luggage

Projection: Growth of Mahagonny
           Series of quick projections

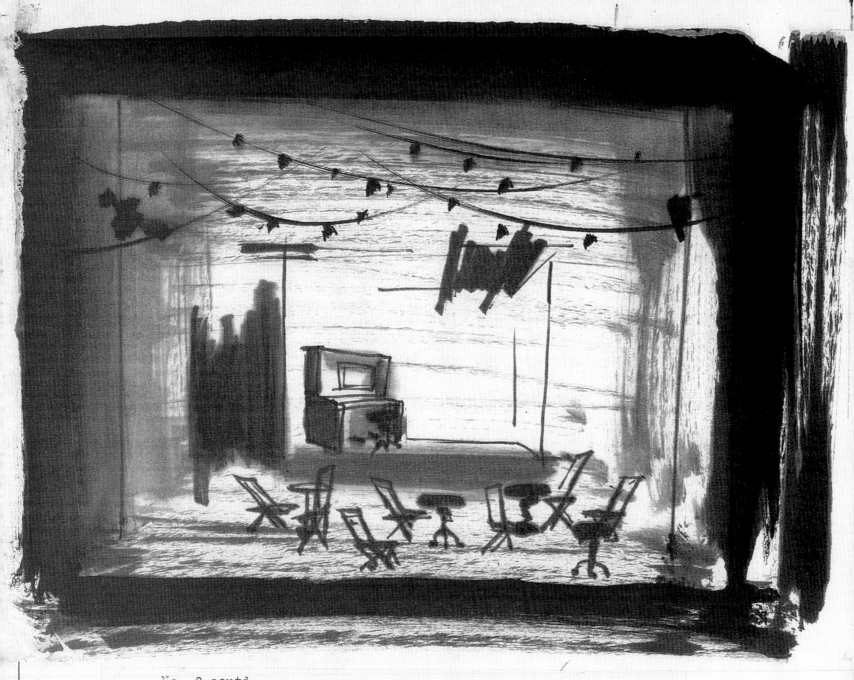

No. 2 contd.

JENNY and six girls enter R over pier
and down steps to line up along front
of stage. They carry suitcases.

ALABAMA Song

Back of stage dark

JENNY and Girls exit L

No. 4 contd.

Tarpaulin has been removed

Rusty corrugated iron structure, but should not
yet be too clearly seen.

Projection contd.

<u>No. 10</u>

<u>Interval</u>

Strike Pole
Structure

Fairy lights go out at opening

'Looting' of everything during this,
leaving only the bare structure standing.

Pros. Natural disasters

<u>No. 11</u>

Same as No.10

At end strike remaining pole structure

Notice:- Proclamation
State of Emergency

ACT II

No. 12

Map Projection on Cyc.

~~Actors~~
Actors huddled on floor etc. watching
course of typhoon.
Only platform remains, nothing else.

The Brothel

Put chairs

Fly out Neon-Sign and strike tables and chairs
~~Leave bench~~ below platform.
Fly in curtain on rod across platform
One chair on platform L of centre for BEGBICK

~~Iron bed behind curtain,~~ curtain open by some
feet in the centre at start, ~~revealing section of be~~
~~and girl.~~

Fly in naked light bulb, behind curtain (?)

desk + chair for Begbick

No. 14 contd.

Crane Song

JENNY)
JIM ⎰   Downstage on opposite sides
         sitting on stools

Darkish upstage.

No. 15

'Fighting'

Fly out curtain (14)

Fly in lights over ' boxing ring'

Set up boxing ring

Brass band on L of Ring.

television bell

No. 16a

Keep lights in over platform

~~Curtain Rod~~ as mast, hoist tablecloth(?) as sail

At end of this strike everything.

(~~Do not turn table as in drawing~~)

Cast climb on top.

~~Set Billiard Table during 'Bindet ihm!'~~
~~in position~~ at front of platform.

No. 19

BENARES Scene

Same as 18

JENNY, BEGBICK, MOSES, FATTY, TOBBY HIGGINS, BILL,
amid the debris, comics, newspapers, popcorn etc.

<u>No. 21</u>

Electric Chair (convert Judge's Chair
       from previous scene.)

After ' Nein sagten die Maenner....' - Stage dark,
strike chair.

Projection of burning Mahagonny.

BEGBICK? FATTY,MOSES downstage ' Aber dieses ganze
             Mahagonny'

During this convert platform back to truck and
wheel off.

(Keep all litter,debris etc. from Courtroom
 until end of opera.)

119

No. 21 a

PROCESSIONS - Finale.

RECENT WORKS
1997-2003

119
Variations on a theme.
A landscape –
a metaphor for
the dominance of
Lady Macbeth

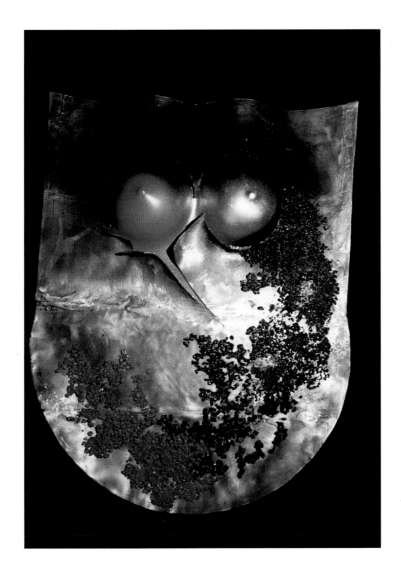

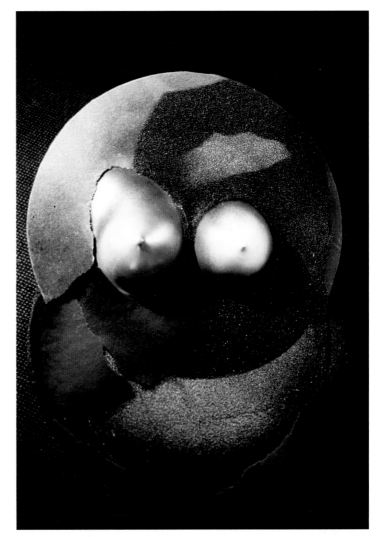

120
Model photograph

121
Model photograph

GENOVEVA
2000

122
Genoveva's vision of freedom on release from wrongful imprisonment.

123
Production photograph

KATYA KABANOVA
2003

124
On the banks of the Volga. Katya imprisoned in the environment – imprisoned mentally.

125
Model photograph

126
Model photograph

127
Production photograph

CHRONOLOGY OF WORK

Ch = Choreographer
Dir = Director

1950
Angélique, Jacques Ibert
Dir: Geoffrey Dunn, London Opera Club

Le Pauvre Matelot, Darius Milhaud
Dir: Joan Cross, London Opera Club

1951
The Sleeping Children, Brian Easdale
Dir: Basil Coleman, English Opera Group

The Wandering Scholar, Gustav Holst
Dir: Basil Coleman, English Opera Group

Werther, Jules Massenet
Dir: Joan Cross, Dartington Hall

1952
Samson and Delilah, Camille Saint-Saëns
Dir: Basil Coleman, Sadler's Wells Theatre

1954
The Boatswain's Mate, Ethel Smyth
Dir: Joan Cross, Dartington Hall

The Governess
St Pancras Town Hall

The Junior Clerk, Sir Lennox Berkeley
Ch: Deryk Mendel, Ballet Comique

1955
Così Fan Tutte, Wolfgang Amadeus Mozart
Dir: Joan Cross, Dartington Hall

Tannhäuser, Richard Wagner
Dir: Sumner Austin, Royal Opera House, Covent Garden

1956
The Marriage of Figaro, Wolfgang Amadeus Mozart
Dir: Joan Cross, Opera School, London

The Medium, Giancarlo Menotti
Dir: Joan Cross, Opera School, London

1957
Samson and Delilah, Camille Saint-Saëns
Dir: Powell Lloyd, Sadler's Wells Theatre

Sister Angelica, Giacomo Puccini
Dir: Joan Cross, Opera School, London

1958
The Judgement of Paris, Hugh Laing and Kurt Weill
Dir: Joan Cross, Opera School, London
Two Brothers, Ernö Dohnányi
Ch: Norman Morrice, Ballet Rambert

1959
Il Campanello, Ermanno Wolf-Ferrari
Dir: Anthony Besch, Opera School, London

Comedy on a Bridge, Bohuslav Martinů
Dir: Joan Cross, Opera School, London

Hazaña, Carlos Surinach
Ch: Norman Morrice, Ballet Rambert

The Impressario, Wolfgang Amadeus Mozart
Dir: Joan Cross, Opera School, London

Iphigenia in Aulis, Christoph Willibald von Gluck
Dir: Joan Cross, Opera School, London

Il Prigoniero, Luigi Dallapiccola
Dir: Anthony Besch, New Opera Company, Sadler's Wells Theatre

Riders to the Sea, Ralph Vaughan Williams
Dir: Joan Cross, Opera School, London

1960
Dido and Aeneas, Henry Purcell
Dir: Joan Cross, Opera School, London

Erwartung, Arnold Schoenberg
Dir: Colin Graham, New Opera Company, Sadler's Wells Theatre

Hercules, Christoph Willibald von Gluck
Dir: Anthony Besch, Handel Opera Society

Il Mondo della Luna, Franz Joseph Haydn
Group 8, St Pancras Town Hall

1961
Carmen, Georges Bizet
Dir: John Barton, Sadler's Wells Theatre

A Place in the Desert, Carlos Surinach
Ch: Norman Morrice, Ballet Rambert

Volpone, Burt
Dir: Michael Geliot, New Opera Company, Sadler's Wells Theatre

1962
Boulevard Solitude, Hans Werner Henze
Dir: Michael Geliot, New Opera Company, Sadler's Wells Theatre

The Caucasian Chalk Circle, Bertolt Brecht
Dir: William Gaskill, Royal Shakespeare Company

Conflicts, Ernest Bloch
Ch: Norman Morrice, Ballet Rambert

A Midsummer Night's Dream, Benjamin Britten
Dir: Basil Coleman, Teatro Colon, Buenos Aires

Murder in the Cathedral, Ildebrando Pizzetti
Sadler's Wells Theatre

The Raising of Lazarus, from the Fleury Playbook
Dir: Brian Trowell, New Opera Company, Sadler's Wells Theatre

Il Tabarro, Giacomo Puccini
Dir: Douglas Craig, Sadler's Wells Theatre

Tales of Hoffman, Jacques Offenbach
Dir: Colin Graham, Opera School, London

1963
Attila, Guiseppe Verdi
Dir: John Blatchley, Sadler's Wells Theatre

Fra Diavolo, Daniel Auber
Dir: Joan Cross, Opera School, London

The Representative, Rolf Hochhuth
Dir: Clifford Williams, Royal Shakespeare Company

The Rise and Fall of the City of Mahagonny, Kurt Weill
Dir: Michael Geliot, Sadler's Wells Theatre

Shout for Life, Terence Feely
Dir: Colin Graham, Vaudeville Theatre, London

The Travellers, Leonard Salzedo
Ch: Norman Morrice, Ballet Rambert

Volo di Notte, Luigi Dallapiccola
Dir: Peter Ebert, Scottish Opera, Glasgow

1964
The Birthday Party, Harold Pinter
Dir: Harold Pinter, Royal Shakespeare Company

Cul de Sac, Christopher Whelen
Ch: Norman Morrice, Ballet Rambert

Don Giovanni, Wolfgang Amadeus Mozart
Dir: Peter Ebert, Scottish Opera

Endgame, Samuel Beckett
Dir: Donald McWhinnie, Royal Shakespeare Company

Happy End, Bertolt Brecht
Edinburgh Festival

The Jew of Malta, Christopher Marlowe
Dir: Clifford Williams, Royal Shakespeare
Company

The Man Who Let It Rain, Brandel
Dir: Herbert Wise, Theatre Royal, Stratford East,
London

Otello, Guiseppe Verdi
Dir: Anthony Besch, Scottish Opera

1965
Boris Godunov, Modest Mussorgsky
Dir: Michael Geliot, Scottish Opera

Don Giovanni, Wolfgang Amadeus Mozart
Dir: Peter Ebert, Los Angeles

From the House of the Dead, Leoš Janáček
Dir: Colin Graham, Sadler's Wells Theatre

The Merchant of Venice, William Shakespeare
Dir: Clifford Williams, Royal Shakespeare
Company

Raymonda, Nureyev after Marius Petipa
Ch: Rudolf Nureyev, Australian Ballet

Timon of Athens, William Shakespeare
Dir: John Schlesinger, Royal Shakespeare
Company

The Tribute, Roger Sessions
Ch: Norman Morrice, Royal Ballet touring company

1966
Allergy, Jonathan Taylor
Dir: Michael Geliot, London Traverse Company

The Bellow Plays, Saul Bellow
Dir: Michael Geliot, London Traverse Company

Bread and Butter, Norman O'Neill
Dir: Michael Geliot, London Traverse Company

Diversities, Henk Badings
Dir: Jonathan Taylor, Ballet Rambert

Gaiety of Nations, Deems Taylor
Dir: Michael Geliot, London Traverse Company

The General's Tea Party, Boris Vian
Dir: Michael Geliot, London Traverse Company

The King's Mare, Canolle, adapted by Loos
Dir: Peter Coe, Garrick Theatre, London

1967
As You Like It, William Shakespeare
Dir: Clifford Williams, National Theatre, London

Little Murders, Jules Feiffer
Dir: Christopher Morahan, Royal Shakespeare
Company

The Rake's Progress, Igor Fedorovich Stravinsky
Dir: Peter Ebert, Scottish Opera

1968
The Drummer's Boy
Dir: Clifford Williams, Alexander Theatre, Toronto

Little Murders, Jules Feiffer
Dir: Clifford Williams, Alexander Theatre, Toronto

Othello, William Shakespeare
Dir: Clifford Williams, Ivan Vasov, Sofia

Raymonda, Nureyev after Marius Petipa
Ch: Rudolf Nureyev, De Norske Opera

Soldiers, Rolf Hochhuth
Dir: Clifford Williams, Alexander Theatre, Toronto;
Albery Theatre, London

The Tempest, William Shakespeare
Dir: John Clements, Chichester Festival Theatre

1969
Back to Methuselah, George Bernard Shaw
Dir: Clifford Williams, National Theatre,
Old Vic, London

1970
The Bacchae, Euripides
Dir: Jean Pierre Ponelle, Schauspielhaus,
Dusseldorf

Elegy for Young Lovers, Hans Werner Henze
Dir: Hans Werner Henze, Scottish Opera

Major Barbara, George Bernard Shaw
Dir: Clifford Williams, Royal Shakespeare
Company

The Valkyrie, Richard Wagner
Dir: Glen Byam Shaw and John Blatchley,
English National Opera, London

1971
Don Giovanni, Wolfgang Amadeus Mozart
Dir: Ian Watt-Smith, Scottish Opera

Götterdämmerung, Richard Wagner
Dir: Glen Byam Shaw and John Blatchley,
English National Opera, London

Lulu, Alban Berg
Dir: Michael Geliot, Welsh National Opera

The Rake's Progress, Igor Fedorovich Stravinsky
Dir: David Pountney, Scottish Opera

1972
Duke Bluebeard's Castle, Béla Bartók
Dir: Glen Byam Shaw, English National Opera,
London

Hullaballoo, a revue
Dir: Frank Dunlop, Criterion Theatre, London

Macbett, Eugène Ionesco
Dir: Gerhard Klingenberg, Burgtheater, Vienna

The Rhinegold, Richard Wagner
Dir: Glen Byam Shaw, English National Opera,
London

Taverner, Peter Maxwell Davies
Dir: Michael Geliot, Royal Opera House, London

1973
Lulu, Alban Berg
Dir: Michael Geliot, Musiktheater, Kassel

Siegfried, Richard Wagner
Dir: Glen Byam Shaw and John Blatchley,
English National Opera, London

Tannhäuser, Richard Wagner
Dir: Bernd Benthaak, Sydney Opera House

Tristan and Isolde, Richard Wagner
Dir: Michael Geliot, Scottish Opera

Wozzeck, Alban Berg
Dir: Michael Geliot, Nederlandische Opera,
Amsterdam

1974
Billy, adapted from *Billy Liar* by Willis Hall and Keith
Waterhouse
Dir: Patrick Garland, Theatre Royal, Drury Lane,
London

Fidelio, Ludwig van Beethoven
Dir: Michael Geliot, Bavarian State Opera, Munich

The Highwayman, Friedrich Schiller
Dir: Hovhanness J. Pilikian, The Roundhouse,
London

Oedipus Tyrannus, Sophocles
Dir: Hovhanness J. Pilikian,
Chichester Festival Theatre

The Ring Cycle, Richard Wagner
Dir: Glen Byam Shaw and John Blatchley,
English National Opera touring company

1975
Don Giovanni, Wolfgang Amadeus Mozart
Dir: Jeremy Sutcliffe, Scottish Opera

The Mouth Organ, devised by the company
Royal Shakespeare Company

Otello, Guiseppe Verdi
Dir: Anthony Besch, Scottish Opera

Too True to be Good, George Bernard Shaw
Dir: Clifford Williams, Royal Shakespeare Company

1976
Billy, adapted from *Billy Liar* by Willis Hall and
Keith Waterhouse
Dir: Patrick Garland, Theater an der Wien, Vienna

Don Giovanni, Wolfgang Amadeus Mozart
Dir: David Pountney, Scottish Opera

Macbeth, Guiseppe Verdi
Dir: David Pountney, Scottish Opera

The Midsummer Marriage, Sir Michael Tippett
Dir: Ian Watt Smith, Welsh National Opera

Old World, Alexei Arbuzov
Dir: Terry Hands, Royal Shakespeare Company

Wild Oats, John O'Keeffe
Dir: Clifford Williams, Royal Shakespeare
Company

1977
Cruel Garden, Carlos Miranda
Ch: Christopher Bruce and Lindsay Kemp,
Ballet Rambert

Don Giovanni, Wolfgang Amadeus Mozart
Dir: Peter Ebert, Scottish Opera

Every Good Boy Deserves Favour, Tom Stoppard
Dir: Trevor Nunn, Royal Festival Hall

The Ice Break, Sir Michael Tippett
Dir: Sam Wanamaker, Royal Opera House,
Covent Garden

King Lear, William Shakespeare
Dir: Hovhanness J. Pilikian, Reykjavik

Macbeth, Guiseppe Verdi
Dir: David Pountney, Scottish Opera

Rosmersholm, Henrik Ibsen
Dir: Clifford Williams, Haymarket Theatre, London

She Stoops to Conquer, Oliver Goldsmith
Dir: Clifford Williams, Hong Kong Festival

Sons of Light, David Rudkin
Dir: Ron Daniels, Royal Shakespeare Company

State of Revolution, Robert Bolt
Dir: Christopher Morahan, National Theatre,
London

1978
Brand, Henrik Ibsen
Dir: Christopher Morahan, National Theatre,
London

The Guardsman, Antal Molnar
Dir: Peter Wood, National Theatre, London

Happy Days, Samuel Beckett
Dir: Philip Haas, Hong Kong Festival

Love's Labour's Lost, William Shakespeare
Dir: John Barton, Royal Shakespeare Company

The Seven Deadly Sins, Kurt Weill
Dirs: Richard Allston and Michael Geliot,
English National Opera, London

The Tempest, William Shakespeare
Dir: Clifford Williams, Royal Shakespeare
Company

1979
Baal, Bertolt Brecht
Dir: David Jones, Royal Shakespeare Company

Don Quixote, adapted from Miguel de Cervantes
Saavedra
Dir: Tom Hawkes, The Roundhouse, London

Hippolytus, David Rudkin
Dir: Ron Daniels, Royal Shakespeare Company

Richard III, William Shakespeare
Dir: Christopher Morahan, National Theatre,
London

The Threepenny Opera, Bertolt Brecht
Dir: Clifford Williams, Aalborg Theatre, Denmark

The Wild Duck, Henrik Ibsen
Dir: Christopher Morahan, National Theatre, London

1980
The Love Girl and the Innocent, Aleksandr
Isayevich Solzhenitsyn
Dir: Clifford Williams, Aalborg Theatre, Denmark

Romeo and Juliet, William Shakespeare
Dir: Ron Daniels, Royal Shakespeare Company

1981
Anna Karenina, Iain Hamilton
Dir: Colin Graham, English National Opera,
London

The Carmelites, Francis Poulenc
Dir: Clifford Williams, Aalborg Theatre, Denmark

Hamlet, William Shakespeare
Dir: John Barton, Royal Shakespeare Company

The Love Girl and the Innocent, Aleksandr
Isayevich Solzhenitsyn
Dir: Clifford Williams, Royal Shakespeare
Company

Man and Superman, George Bernard Shaw
Dir: Christopher Morahan, National Theatre,
London

Romeo and Juliet, William Shakespeare
Dir: Ron Daniels, Royal Shakespeare Company

Terra Nova, Ted Tally
Dir: Clifford Williams, Aalborg Theatre, Denmark

1982
Don Giovanni, Wolfgang Amadeus Mozart
Dir: Michael Geliot, Welsh National Opera

Façade, Sir William Walton and Dame Edith Sitwell
Dir: John Woolf, Royal Shakespeare Company and
London Symphony Orchestra

Molière, Mikhail Bulgakov
Dir: Bill Alexander, Royal Shakespeare Company

Much Ado About Nothing, William Shakespeare
Dir: Terry Hands, Royal Shakespeare Company

The Soldier's Tale, Igor Fedorovich Stravinsky
Dir: Tony Church, Royal Shakespeare Company
and London Symphony Orchestra

1983
Bugsy Malone, Paul Williams, adapted by
Michael Dolenz
Dir: Michael Dolenz, Her Majesty's Theatre,
London

The Custom of the Country, Nicholas Wright
Dir: David Jones, Royal Shakespeare Company

Cyrano de Bergerac, Edmond Rostand
Dir: Terry Hands, Royal Shakespeare Company

Dear Anyone, Jack Rosenthal
Dir: David Taylor, Cambridge Theatre, London

Pack of Lies, Hugh Whitemore
Dir: Clifford Williams, Lyric Theatre, London

Die Soldaten, Bernd Alois Zimmermann
Dir: Ken Russell, Lyons Opera

1984
Cyrano de Bergerac, Edmond Rostand
Dir: Terry Hands, Royal Shakespeare Company
(video film)

Italian Girl in Algiers, Gioacchino Rossini
Dir: Ken Russell, Grand Théâtre de Genève

Much Ado About Nothing, William Shakespeare
Dir: Terry Hands, Royal Shakespeare Company

Pack of Lies, Hugh Whitemore
Dir: Michael Reddington, Lyric Theatre, London

The Rise and Fall of the City of Mahagonny,
Kurt Weill
Dir: Clifford Williams, Aalborg Theatre, Denmark

1985
Anna Karenina, Iain Hamilton
Dir: Colin Graham, English National Opera

Measure for Measure, William Shakespeare
Dir: Clifford Williams, Norrkoping, Sweden

Othello, William Shakespeare
Dir: Terry Hands, Royal Shakespeare Company

Pack of Lies, Hugh Whitemore
Dir: Clifford Williams, Hamburg, Boston, New York

Tribute to Michael Redgrave
Dir: Anthony Page, Old Vic Theatre, London

Troilus and Cressida, William Shakespeare
Dir: Howard Davies, Royal Shakespeare Company

1986
Across from the Garden of Allah, Charles Wood
Dir: Ron Daniels, Comedy Theatre, London

Tannhäuser, Richard Wagner
Dir: Martha Galvin, Grand Théâtre de Genève

1987
The Flying Dutchman, Richard Wagner
Dir: Ralph Koltai, Hong Kong Arts Festival

Pacific Overtures, Stephen Sondheim
Dir: Keith Warner, English National Opera

They Shoot Horses Don't They?, Horace McCoy
and Ray Herman
Dir: Ron Daniels, Royal Shakespeare Company,
Mermaid Theatre

1988
Carrie, adapted by Lawrence Cohen from
Stephen King's novel
Dir: Terry Hands, Royal Shakespeare Company

Cruel Garden, Carlos Miranda
Ch: Christopher Bruce and Lindsay Kemp,
English National Ballet

The Seagull, Anton Chekov
Dir: Charles Marowitz, LA Theatre Center,
Los Angeles

1989
Metropolis, adapted from Fritz Lang's film
Dir: Jerome Savary, Piccadilly Theatre, London

1990
E.A.R.W.I.G., Paula Milne
Dir: Ron Daniels, Royal Shakespeare Company

The Planets, Gustav Holst
Ch: David Bintley, Royal Opera House, Covent
Garden, London

La Traviata, Guiseppe Verdi
Dir: Ralph Koltai, Hong Kong Arts Festival

1991
The Makropulos Affair, Leoš Janáček
Dir: Keith Warner, Norwegian Opera, Oslo

1992
Cruel Garden, Carlos Miranda
Ch: Christopher Bruce and Lindsay Kemp,
Berlin Staatsoper

1993
Cruel Garden, Carlos Miranda
Ch: Christopher Bruce and Lindsay Kemp,
Houston Ballet

Hair, James Rado with Gerome Ragni
Dir: Michael Bogdanov, Old Vic Theatre

My Fair Lady, Alan Jay Lerner, Frederick Loewe
and Moss Hart
Dir: Howard Davies, New York

La Traviata, Guiseppe Verdi
Dir: Knut Hendriksen, Stockholm

1994
Otello, Gioacchino Rossini
Dir: Michael Bogdanov, Opera House, Essen

1995
Madam Butterfly, Giacomo Puccini
Dir: David Pountney, Bunkamura, Tokyo

1996
The House of Bernarda Alba, Federico Garcia
Lorca
Dir: Di Trevis, Teatr Clwyd

Twelfth Night, William Shakespeare
Dir: Søm Iversen, Royal Theatre, Copenhagen

1997
Carmen, Georges Bizet
Dir: Frank Dunlop, Royal Albert Hall, London

Simon Boccanegra, Guiseppe Verdi
Dir: David Pountney, Welsh National Opera

Timon of Athens, William Shakespeare
Dir: Michael Bogdanov, Shakespeare Repertory
Theatre, Chicago

1998
Suddenly Last Summer, Tennessee Williams
Dir: Ralph Koltai, Nottingham Playhouse

Nabucco, Guiseppe Verdi
Dir: Stefano Vizioli, Corégie Orange

Dalibor, Smetana
Dir: David Pountney, Scottish Opera, Edinburgh
Festival

A Midsummer Night's Dream, William Shakespeare
Dir: Flemming Enevold, Gladsaxe Theatre,
Copenhagen

Macbeth, William Shakespeare
Copenhagen

1999
Don Giovanni, Wolfgang Amadeus Mozart
Dir: Johannes Schaaf, Marynski Theatre,
St Petersburg

2000
Genoveva, Robert Schumann
Dir: David Pountney, Opera North

2003
Katya Kabanova, Leoš Janáček
Dir: David Pountney, La Fenice, Venice

Simon Boccanegra, Guiseppe Verdi
Dir: David Pountney, Tel Aviv Opera

CHRONOLOGY

31 July 1924	Born in Berlin.
1939	Granted British entry visa.
1945-7	Served in the Royal Army Service Corps and with British Intelligence.
1948-51	Studied at Central School of Arts and Crafts and obtained a Diploma with Distinction.
1963-6	Associate Designer with the Royal Shakespeare Company.
1965-72	Head of Department of Theatre Design, Central School of Art and Design.
1967	London Drama Critics Award, Designer of the Year, for *As You Like It* and *Little Murders*.
1975	Gold Medal for Stage Design, Prague Quadriennale International Exhibition of Scenography.
1976-present	Associate Designer with the Royal Shakespeare Company.
1978	Society of West End Theatres Designer of the Year Award for *Brand*.
1979	'Golden Triga' National Award, Prague Quadriennale International Exhibition of Scenography.
1981	London Drama Critics Award for *The Love Girl and the Innocent*.
1983	Awarded Commander of the Order of the British Empire (CBE).
1984	Elected Royal Designer for Industry (RDI) of the Royal Society of Arts.
1984	Society of West End Theatres Designer of the Year Award for *Cyrano de Bergerac*.
1987	Silver Medal for Stage Design, Prague Quadriennale International Exhibition of Scenography.
1991	'Golden Triga' National Award, Prague Quadriennale International Exhibition of Scenography.
1993	Special Award for Distinguished Service to Theatre, United States Institute of Theatre Technology (USITT).
1994	Elected Fellow of the Academy of Performing Arts, Hong Kong.
1996	Elected Honorary Fellow of the London Institute.
1997	Retrospective Exhibition at the Lethaby Galleries, London Institute.
1998-99	Retrospective Exhibitions, Beijing, Hong Kong, Taipei.
1999	Elected Fellow of the Rose Bruford College, London.
2003	'Golden Triga' National Award, Prague Quadriennale International Exhibition of Scenography.

BIBLIOGRAPHY

Bablet, Denis, *The Revolution of Stage Design in the Twentieth Century*, Leon Amiel Publishers, Paris, 1977.

Burian, Jarka, 'Ralph Koltai'; in Colin Naylor (ed.) *Contemporary Designers*, St James Press, London, 1996.

Farley, Peter, 'A Stage of Creation'; in Peter Docherty and Tim White (eds), *Design for Performance: from Diaghilev to the Pet Shop Boys*, Lund Humphries Publishers and The Lethaby Press, London, 1996.

Fingleton, David, 'Interview: Ralph Koltai', *Arts Review*, 16 March 1979, vol.31, no.5.

Goodwin, John (ed.), *British Theatre Design: the Modern Age*, Weidenfeld and Nicholson, London, 1989.

Hainaux, René and Yves Bonat (eds), *Stage Design throughout the World since 1960*, Éditions Meddens, Brussels, 1972.

Herbert, Ian (ed.), *Who's Who in the Theatre*, Pitman, London, 1977.

Kane, Angela, 'Rambert: doubling back to the sixties', *Dance Theatre Journal*, Autumn 1990, vol.8, part 3, pp.34-7.

Koltai, Ralph, 'Design and a game of psychology: Ralph Koltai in conversation with Anthony Masters', *Plays and Players*, April 1983, no.355, pp.16-18.

Koltai, Ralph, 'Theatre design: the exploration of space', *Journal of the Royal Society of Arts*, March 1987, vol.135, no.5368, pp.298, 301-9.

Koltai, Ralph, a statement accompanying his entry in Colin Naylor (ed.), *Contemporary Designers*, St James Press, London, 1996.

Lavender, Andy, 'Blood and sex by the bucketful: an interview with Ralph Koltai', *The Times*, 4 February 1997.

Loney, Glen, 'If it burns forget it: an interview with Ralph Koltai', *Theatre Crafts*, January/February 1977.

'The Magnificent Seven: seven U.K. participants in the 1991 Prague Quadriennale including Ralph Koltai give their views', *Sightline*, August 1991, vol.25, part 3, pp.10-11.

McAlhone, Beryl, 'The Extraordinary Stage Design of Ralph Koltai', interview in *Design and Art*, March 1983.

O'Brien, Timothy and David Fingleton, essays in *British Theatre Design 1983-87*, an exhibition catalogue, Society of British Theatre Designers and Twyman Publishing, Farringdon, 1987.

Polan, Brenda, 'Quick change of scene: Brenda Polan meets Ralph Koltai, designer of *Brand*', *The Guardian*, 26 April 1978.

Runciman, Rosy, 'Opera design history looks at Ralph Koltai', *Opera Now*, July/August 1977, pp.38-40.

Schouvaloff, Alexander, *Theatre on Paper*, Sotheby's in association with The Drawing Center, New York, 1990.

Shakespeare, William, *The Tempest*: with eight designs by Ralph Koltai created for the Chichester Festival production 1968, The Folio Society, London, 1971.

Smuthwaite, Nick, 'According to Koltai', *Design Week*, May 1987, vol.2, no.17, pp.20-21.

Truss, Lynn, 'Keeping the curtain up: interview with Ralph Koltai', *The Times*, 24 June 1985.

White, Tim, 'Pushing the Boundaries: Advancing the Dance', in *The Designers: pushing the boundaries: advancing the dance*, catalogue for an exhibition at The Lethaby Gallery, Central Saint Martins College of Art and Design, London, 1995.

Wolfe, Debbie, 'Design for acting', *Drama*, 1986, vol.3, no.161, pp.13-14.

CONTRIBUTORS

Sylvia Backemeyer

Sylvia Backemeyer, the editor, is Director of Learning Resources at Central Saint Martins College of Art and Design. Her role includes work on exhibitions and publications. She has edited two books for Lund Humphries and the Lethaby Press to accompany college exhibitions: *W. R. Lethaby 1857-1931: Architecture, Design and Education* (with Teresa Gronberg) 1984, and *Object Lessons: Central Saint Martins Art and Design Archive*, 1996.

Mike Barnett

As a Chartered Mechanical Engineer, Mike Barnett's skill with hydraulic, pneumatic and electrical controls has proved invaluable in realising the ideas of designers such as Koltai. He has worked for the National Theatre, the Barbican Centre and the Royal Opera House. Freelance since 1978 he has been responsible for the engineering of many productions, including, for Ralph Koltai, *Metropolis*, *The Ring*, *The Planets* and *Simon Boccanegra*.

Pamela Howard

Professor Pamela Howard has worked as a designer for the Royal Shakespeare Company, the Royal National Theatre, the West Yorkshire Playhouse, the Birmingham Repertory Theatre and for television. She is the founder and director of the Central Saint Martins MA in Scenography based in Prague, Helsinki, Utrecht and London. She has made a significant contribution to the study of theatre design. Her book *Scenography* is to be published shortly in the Theatre in Context series. Her work as a director includes *Celestina* (Almeida Theatre) and *Shakespeare's Universe* (the Barbican).

Norman Morrice

Norman Morrice was a member of Ballet Rambert and met Ralph Koltai in 1958 when he was choreographing his first ballet, *Two Brothers*. This collaboration was followed by *Hazaña*, *A Place in the Desert*, *Conflicts*, *The Travellers*, and *Cul-de-Sac*. In 1966 Morrice became an Associate Director of the Ballet Rambert and Koltai, then Head of Theatre Design at the Central School, invited him to use the newly-built Jeanetta Cochrane Theatre as the company's London base. From 1977 to 1986 he was Artistic Director of the Royal Ballet at Covent Garden. He is now Director of the Royal Ballet Choreographic Group and teaches at the Royal Ballet School.

John Napier

As the designer of *Cats, Starlight Express, Les Misérables, Miss Saigon* and *Sunset Boulevard*, John Napier's work is known worldwide. He trained at Central School of Arts and Crafts under Ralph Koltai and is an Associate Designer for the Royal Shakespeare Company, where he designed *Nicholas Nickleby*. His work at the National includes Peter Shaffer's *Equus*. His opera credits include *Lohengrin* and *Macbeth* for the Royal Opera. He created the spectacular *Siegfried and Roy Show* in Las Vegas, and his film work includes Steven Spielberg's *Hook*. He has two SWET awards, an Olivier, a BAFTA, and five Tonys.

Trevor Nunn

In 1962 Trevor Nunn won the ABC Director's Scholarship to the Belgrade Theatre Coventry. He joined the Royal Shakespeare Company in 1964, became Associate Director in 1965, and the company's youngest-ever Artistic Director in 1968. From 1978 to 1986, he was joint Artistic Director with Terry Hands. He has directed many productions for the RSC and co-directed *Nicholas Nickleby,* winner of five Tonys and *Les Misérables* which won eight and is the most performed musical in the world. In 1982 he opened the RSC's new London home, the Barbican Theatre, and the Swan Theatre at Stratford in 1986. He has directed several award-winning musicals for Andrew Lloyd Webber, and operas at Glyndebourne. He is a past Artistic Director of the Royal National Theatre.

Tim White

Dr White was Research Assistant for the Design for Performance Research Project at Central Saint Martins from 1994 to 1997. He co-curated the exhibition *The Designers: Pushing the Boundaries, Advancing the Dance* held in the Lethaby Galleries in 1995, and co-authored its catalogue. Together with the Project Director, Peter Docherty, he edited *Design for Performance: From Diaghilev to the Pet Shop Boys*, published by Lund Humphries and the Lethaby Press, 1996.